This Walker book
belongs to:

_____

_____

_____

For Emma, Chris and Arthur x
L. D.

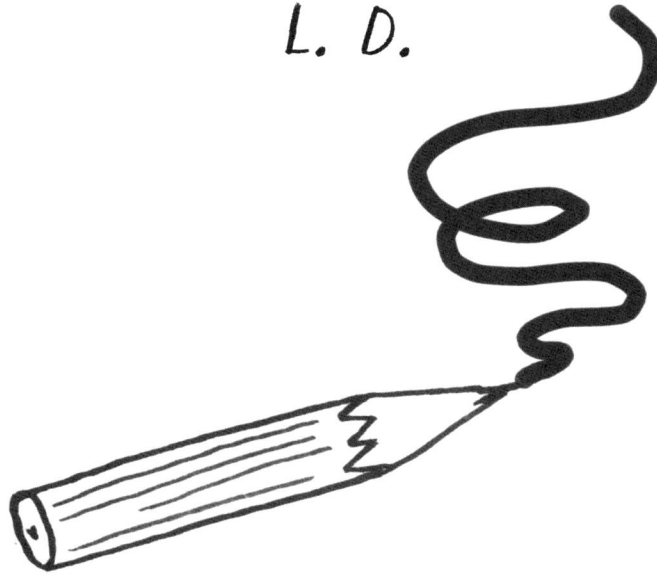

For Fiadh, Bláithín Grace, Éabha
and Fíadh Mc x
A. L.

With thanks to Lucy Blair

First published 2025 by Walker Books Ltd, 87 Vauxhall Walk, London SE11 5HJ

2 4 6 8 10 9 7 5 3 1

Text © 2025 Laura Dockrill • Illustrations © 2025 Ashling Lindsay

The right of Laura Dockrill and Ashling Lindsay to be identified as author and illustrator respectively of this work has been asserted in accordance with the Copyright, Designs and Patents Act 1988

EU Authorized Representative: HackettFlynn Ltd, 36 Cloch Choirneal, Balrothery, Co. Dublin, K32 C942, Ireland
EU@walkerpublishinggroup.com

This book has been typeset in Intro

Printed in China

British Library Cataloguing in Publication Data: a catalogue record for this book is available from the British Library

ISBN 978-1-5295-0350-0

www.walker.co.uk

BIG THOUGHTS

Catch and Release Your Worries

LAURA
DOCKRILL

ASHLING
LINDSAY

WALKER BOOKS
AND SUBSIDIARIES
LONDON • BOSTON • SYDNEY • AUCKLAND

Today I feel like myself.

And when I feel like myself, *nothing* can stop me!
My mind is full of my favourite things:
Sunshine on my face.
The first footprints in the snow.
Shooting stars.

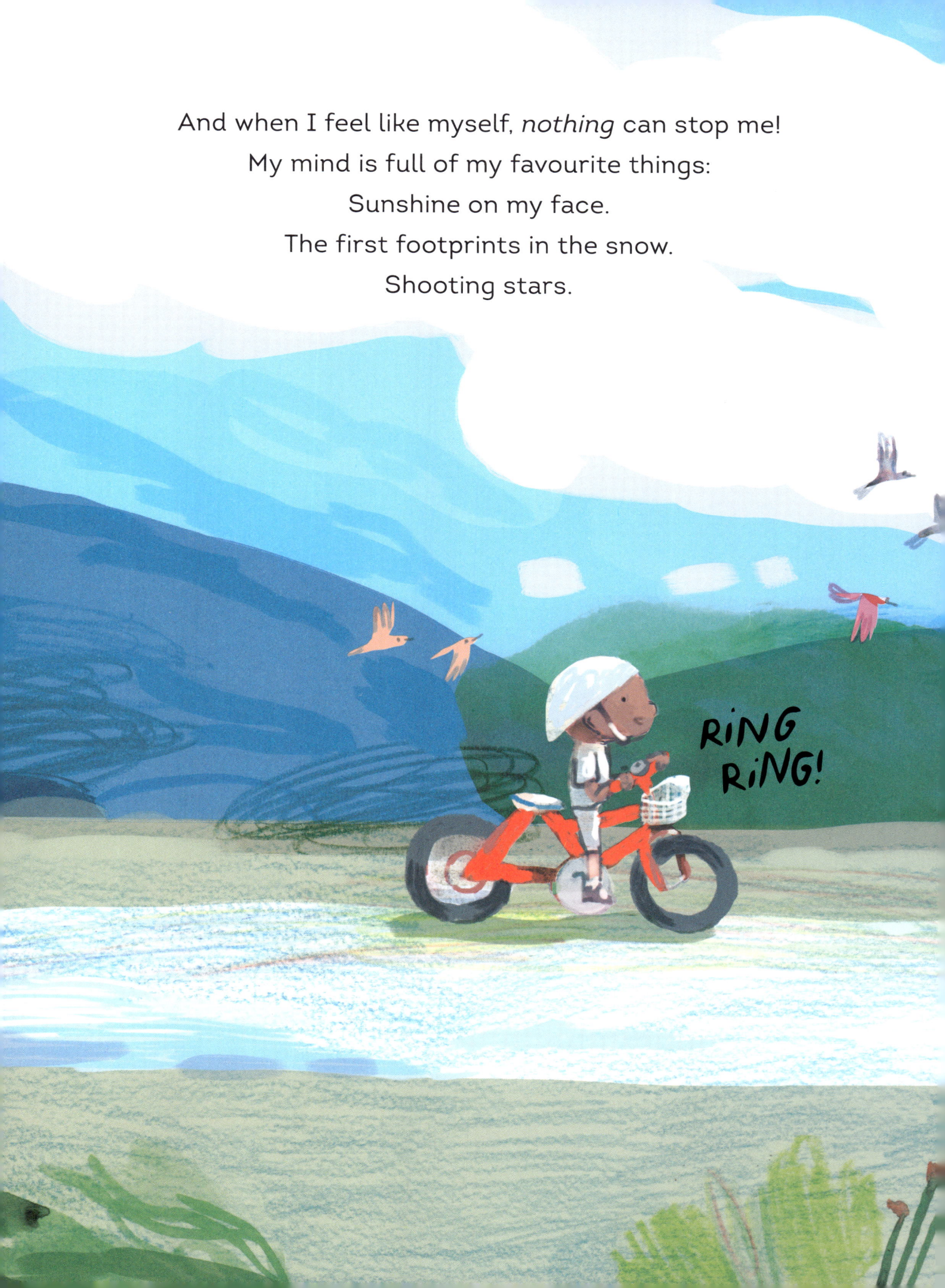

RING RING!

A flock of pink birds in the sky.
Jelly beans in a jar.
A sharpened pencil.
A bicycle (with a bell, *obviously*). RING RING!

But then there are times when I don't feel like myself.

In these wobbly moments, my belly feels sick,
my heart thumps, and sometimes I even want to cry.
I don't want to do *anything*.
I won't even eat a jelly bean (and I can always eat jelly beans).
And that's because of my **Big Thoughts**.
That's what I call my worries.

Big Thoughts are invisible. Nobody else
can see the way they make me feel.

Big Thoughts are loud. Nobody else
can hear the racket they make!

Big Thoughts can be about the future:
I worry about things that haven't happened
and might not *ever* happen!

Big Thoughts can be about the past.
I worry about things I said or did.

Big Thoughts can even be make-believe.
That's one of the annoying things about **Big Thoughts**.
They don't always tell the truth.

I try to ignore **Big Thoughts**.
La-la-la-la, I'm not listening.
But the more I try to get rid
of them, the louder they get.

I try to run from **Big Thoughts**, but wherever I go,
the **Big Thoughts** come too.

Oh, no, not you again.

I wish I had the power
to make them go away!

Although I feel frightened to talk about
the **Big Thoughts** out loud, I don't feel
like I can hold them in any longer.

My big sister, Sky, says, "Take a deep breath, Sonny.
The reason we take a breath is
to let our brain know we are not in danger.
We are safe. You are OK. I am here."

So, in a tiny whisper,
I tell Sky about my **Big Thoughts**.

"Thank you for telling me," says Sky.
"Asking for help is the bravest thing a person can do.
You're kind of cool, you know, Sonny?"

And then the **Big Thoughts**
become quieter and lighter.

And it turns out I'm not the only one
who carries around **Big Thoughts** either.

Maybe telling my friend
how I am feeling
is a power?

Because even my friend, who I think
is the coolest, has **Big Thoughts**, too!
And suddenly I don't feel so alone.

Together, my friend and I can sit by a river and let go of
our **Big Thoughts** and watch them drift away.

Just as my sister is kind and calm with me,
I can be kind and calm with myself.

Calming a **Big Thought** is like catching a fish.

First, I catch it. I say,
"Hi."

Then I let it go.

I watch it swim away.

It also helps to remember
all of my favourite things in the world
until I feel like myself again.
Jelly beans in a jar. A sharpened pencil.
A bicycle (with a bell, *obviously*). RING
RING!

RING
RING!

And most of all, being with people I love,
who love me too.

Even if the **Big Thoughts** come back,

I know what to do now. I know I'll be OK.

Tips and Techniques

In this book, Sonny has lots of worries and scary thoughts. Some are imaginary, like the angry tiger and the piranhas, and some are real, like falling off a bike and thunderstorms.

Everybody experiences thoughts and feelings like this. The important thing to remember is that you do not have to carry your worries alone.

Sonny uses a few ways to help manage his Big Thoughts. You can also use some of these techniques to help you feel better.

1 **Speak to someone you trust.** Do you have a family member, a grown-up who you trust or a good friend who makes you feel happy and safe? Why not share your worries with them? Maybe you'll be surprised – they might have the same worries too.

2 **Write the Big Thoughts down.** It helps to write Big Thoughts down so they don't swirl in your head and overwhelm you. Writing allows us to see the thought for what it really is and keeps it simple. (Drawing is great too!)

3 **Start catching your Big Thoughts.** Sonny pictures his scary thoughts as a fish. He imagines catching the fish – the Big Thought – saying "hi" and then letting it go. Here's how you can try it too:

- **CATCH IT!** Catch the Big Thought. Let's say you've recently fallen off your bike and now you are worried about riding your bike again. This is the fish.
- **CHECK IT.** Now try not to see the worry fish as something scary. Instead, look at it closely, like a detective, and ask it questions: What would happen if I fell off my bike again and hurt myself? Or what if people laugh at me? Then ask yourself: Is that a **helpful** thought?
- **CHANGE IT.** Now, by really looking at your Big Thought, you can try to **change it**:
  - ◆ Remind yourself of all the times you *haven't* fallen off your bike.

- Be kind to yourself about the fact that, yes, when you fell off your bike it hurt, but remember that doesn't take away how you're able to get to places speedily and go riding with your friends.
- You can do what is in your control to feel safer – always wear a helmet and take it slow.
- Remind yourself that falling off a bike is a part of riding a bike – it's normal. It's how we learn.
- Then **LET IT GO.** Bye, worry fish!

TIP: It helps me to remember that my worries are not there to hurt me but to keep me safe. I try to feel grateful that they are there instead of angry or upset by them.

4 **Create your own happy box.** Why not get an old shoe box, or any kind of box, and fill it with little things that make you happy? Maybe put in your favourite book, some toys or a photo of someone you love. The box can be full of anything that makes you feel happy to look at or to hold.

5 **Keep busy.** Walking, playing, speaking to a friend, watching your favourite TV show or reading a book are helpful ways to distract yourself. If you can't, that's OK. Try not to be angry at yourself. It's perfectly normal, and eventually you will be able to.

TIP: Helping others is a GREAT way to lift our mood. Try helping your grown-up cook, tidying up or doing an activity with your sibling or friend.

6 **Get a good night's sleep.** Everything feels a lot harder when you're tired. Getting a good night's sleep will make your mind feel calmer, and your worries smaller. If you can't sleep, maybe try reading a book or comic, listening to music or doing something relaxing like a puzzle before you go to sleep.

TIP: Deal with worries in the day, not at bedtime. Maybe set a "worry time" and decide that that's the only time you can worry. Bedtime is your peaceful place.

Remember, you cannot change something that has already happened – don't worry about things you could have done differently or things you feel you should have said.

Life does not always go as planned. You can't be happy all the time, and that is healthy.

And always ask for help – it's the bravest thing a person can do.

Things that make Laura happy:

Day trips with my family

Playing with my wild kitten, Sunflower
(but she is very scratchy)

Reading books

Listening to loud rock music

Wearing bright pink lipstick

Laughing with my friends

Singing to music in the car
(especially when I know all the words)

Bookshops

Mountains of vegetables

Crisps

Tea

Things that make Ashling happy:

The night sky

Laughing with family

Good bread